DINOSAURS

by Grace Maccarone
Illustrated by Richard Courtney

Dinosaurs lived
long ago.

Fossils tell us
what we know.

Some were big.

Some were small.

Some were long.

Some were tall.

Some had beaks.

Some had sails.

Some had plates
and powerful tails.

Some had spikes

or bird-like feet.

Some ate plants.

And some ate meat.

Some had horns and bony frills.

Some had fancy crests and bills.

Some had sharp claws.

Some had strong jaws.

Some dinosaurs
fought each other.

Some of the young stayed
close to mother.

Some dinosaur eggs
hatched in a nest.

Which dinosaur do you like best?

Diplodocus

Ultrasaurus

Saltopus

Tyrannosaurus

Spinosaurus

Struthiomimus

Ankylosaurus

Stegosaurus

Iguanodon

Hypsilophodon

Dryosaurus   Allosaurus

Triceratops

Apatosaurus

Deinonychus

Lambeosaurus

Protoceratops

Velociraptor

Homalocephale

Ceratosaurus

Maiasaura